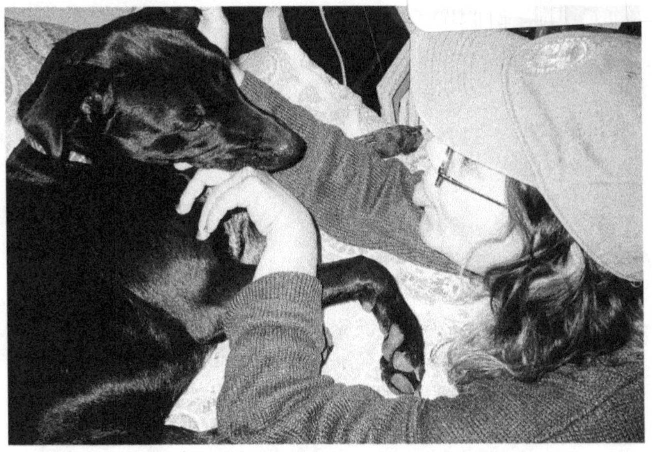

Currently living in San Diego, CA, Gemma Hernandez Serrano is a college student studying sociology and American Indian studies. Over the last decade, her creativity has expressed itself in art. She enjoys reading, gardening, camping, and hiking. When she is not studying, you can find her attending a concert or on her couch binge-watching horror movies.

This book is dedicated to survivors of child abuse.

Gemma Hernandez Serrano

MIDNIGHT

AUSTIN MACAULEY PUBLISHERS™

LONDON • CAMBRIDGE • NEW YORK • SHARJAH

Ordering Information
Quantity sales: Special discounts are available on quantity purchases by corporations, associations, and others. For details, contact the publisher at the address below.

Publisher's Cataloging-in-Publication data
Serrano, Gemma Hernandez
Midnight

ISBN 9781645363446 (Paperback)
ISBN 9781645363439 (Hardback)
ISBN 9781645368939 (ePub e-book)

Library of Congress Control Number: 2020923800

www.austinmacauley.com/us

First Published (2021)
Austin Macauley Publishers LLC
40 Wall Street, 33rd Floor, Suite 3302
New York, NY 10005
USA

mail-usa@austinmacauley.com
+1 (646) 5125767

The poems originally started off as letters meant to quietly hold the turmoil of a changing woman. They soon became an unveiling of understanding as to how my mind processed trauma. I'd lost control and stumbled effortlessly into the dark, quiet corner of my mind. That is until I found my family and community. They unconditionally held my hand as I made my way back through an unfamiliar door. Thank you for patience, love, courage, and friendship. You taught me how to regrow and survive on new roots. This book was dedicated to survivors of abuse not only because I am a survivor of abuse but because I know what it is like to feel alone with that pain. You are not alone anymore, I am proud of you, and I love you. There is so, so much strength and beauty within you. The path to healing will be long and imperfect, remember you don't have to do it alone and that you're allowed to feel joy, wonder, and love. Now close your eyes and take a deep breath. You are here, you are alive, and you are worthy.

National Domestic Violence Hotline: 1 (800) 799-7233
National Child Abuse Hotline: 1 (800) 422-4453
National Suicide Prevention Lifeline: 1 (800) 273-8255

Your Love

Sunblind as you smile warmly in your sleep
I prefer it like this
a cold morning bundled up next to you
in a small town
miles away
spending moments playing house
as if I'll leave before you
as if you'll never leave.

Second Turn to the Left

I'm better off alone
swallowing the rock in my throat
as I make all the wrong turns
thinking to myself
wondering,
if I'm asking
for too much,
again.

Storm

I float,
not toward an island,
but toward you.
I should feel happy
going through
waves, but instead
the water is concrete
and I'm
filled with disappointment.

Tender Greens

His kiss was tender
it was all I imagined
it was the only thing I got
from the first man
that left.

Need

I'm sorry, I keep running.
You've been consistent, but I still find
reasons to hide.

I'm not sure why,
why I'm so afraid
of talking.

All day I lay
staring at walls
watching words
appear in ways
I can't say out loud.

I'm sorry it had to be this way.

With You

I am never good enough
for them to stay
I am never good enough
for them to say
you're mine.

Give Me an Idea

Your mention of her feels heavy on my chest.
I want to tell you,
I want to ask you,
but the question
never leaves my mouth.
Your arms may be around me,
but I know, at the end of the night, in your mind
you'll be holding her.

Spin

My thoughts at night betray me
convince me to settle in
and close my eyes.
To conjure static
from memories of our hands touching.
The smell of pine drifts in,
the heat escapes from my chest
as I imagine laying underneath your flame
even with the distance, I spin
slowly, towards you.

Oatmeal

The pool water
was cold and thick,
like oatmeal
as you placed your hand
between my legs
and everyone watched.

Solar

I can feel you under,
slowly
melting
into
my skin.

Breathing,
it
gets
harder.

You weigh me down,
you
consume
all of me.

Let Me Taste You

Imagine a love so sweet,
it tastes just like honey.
It will stick and spread to every crevice of your heart,
control your limbs and tear you apart.
How am I supposed to empty myself of you?

Loving the Pendulum

If you look for love, you'll fail.
If you say you love, do you really?
In my experience,
we never really love.
How can we look for love, if *we are never love?*
If you look for love, then you don't *know* love.
True love.
you can only find that within yourself,
if you look for love, everyone will know,
that you don't love yourself.
And we never really love, because
we never love the same.
We never stay the same.
the love you have for your friends is different every year.
The love you have for your mother and father is different
every year.
You see, in order to find love
you need to stop looking for love.
You need to start *being* love.

Midnight

We'd lay still, with our hands entwined
on a Friday night.
Pieces of us scattered on the floor
the steady hum of the air conditioner
reminding me of home
as we'd wrap our cold bodies
together for warmth
and lay still, so still.
Until, your voice dripped with poison
and you'd enter me again.

Love

When it comes to love, I tend to live in a fantasy.
So, I can escape truths
that cannot be ignored.
A pattern I create to mistake
hope for lust.
It's meant to end in silence
and names sprawled
across the sky.
That's all I'll ever be,
a thin red line
to forget.
I sift through
the emptiness
I, somehow, find myself
at a steady pace,
falling toward my grave.

Control

I want to hear the way you say my name
not the way white people say it,
but the way it was intended
to be said.
The soft "huh"
that escapes from your mouth
as you finish with the
confidence and fortitude of my Mexica ancestors.
I want to hear you say my name,
not the way coffeeshops say it
with an English "Juh",
forgetting that languages exists beyond their borders.
I want to hear you say my name,
the way my mother screams it when she's angry,
"GEMMA!"
I want to hear you say my name,
followed by an, "I love you."
I want to hear you say my name,
as if it's the last time you will see me.
As if it's the last time you will have control.

Lemonade in the Summer

I am hungry for true love
as if true love
was something I could
find at the corner liquor store.

I am hungry for true love
the kind that keeps his
his hands around my throat.

Lips
sweet like strawberry
lemonade in the summer.

I am hungry for true love
like the movies I watch
on Friday nights
with my dog.

I am so hungry
I am willing to change
the way you say my name.

I am so hungry
I wouldn't mind
pruning my garden
so, it's easier to find.

I wouldn't mind
forgetting what I feel
if it made sleeping
with you real
I wouldn't mind
lemonade in the summer.

Honey

I draw my legs up to my chest
and cradle myself in the dark.

As the shadows come to me,
quivering hands hastily unravel my sanity.
I feel the cold spreading to my chest,
numbing me,
as I try not to hurt.
Why won't it leave me alone?
Mother, I wish you could cover me

I open my mouth, but nothing comes out.
Nothing.
Mother, I wish you could cover me
mother, why won't you cover me?

When I Get Old

When I get old,
I'll know I was a good mother,
because I learned from my own
that there's more to grow
than the body in your womb
I'll trade words of hurt and pain
for those of love and encouragement
and hide insecurities with laughter and joy
and on the days, I see
in black and grey
I won't make it their fault.

Like My Mother

I know I am my mother's daughter
When I shut my mouth
to keep it inside
until my blood gets thick
in ways I didn't want it to.

I know I am my mother's daughter
when I become dependent
unable to catch myself
and placing expectations on unreciprocated love.

I know I am my mother's daughter
when I imagine ways to keep
from telling the truth,
I don't want to be a trained liar.

I know I am my mother's daughter
when I can't make sense
of why I run away
unable to forgive, unable to fix
unable to explain that I
can't figure me out.

I know I'll be my mother's daughter
when I no longer remember
my name.

Hate Her (Hate Me)

I am desperate to feel,
anything but hate,
for the face in the mirror.
If I shut my eyes tightly enough,
I believe I can make it disappear.
A rotten taste builds up in my mouth
and as I spit it out,
I imagine the face,
with its hateful grin,
obsidian blades
jutting out from porcelain white,
slip through, into the dark,
and away from my mind.

Mr. Smiley Face

There are no fingers left
to count the times my body was taken
without my consent
there are no categories left
to define the state of
my womanhood.

Sometimes We Feel

My days pass by, and there I am.
On the floor, staring at the ceiling fan.
Wondering if I'm the only one
dissolving,
dissolving…

Fatherly Love

[What is a father?]
A father doesn't go in your room,
dripping in cheap beer and covered in dust
expecting you to be asleep,
but really
you're frozen in bed
mourning your childhood,
counting your breathes
as he scrapes your insides out.

Blue Sky

I'm feeling blue,
like the sky above your face.
Somehow, I still feel the need
to apologize,
as if I've failed you
for wanting to disappear.

Ghosts

Names are like ghosts
beware of them all
with so many forms
all lit up to see
and the sound of their names,
no matter the change,
are crawling inside
waiting to be free
claw, claw, claw, claw
their way up
and out your throat.
That feeling
that sound
they're haunting.

Generations

I need to remember,

suppressing is not forgetting.

As much as I fight it, as much as I cry about it,

I have yet to overcome,

the haunting revelations passed onto me

from generations,

of violence and pain.

Even in, my moments of clarity

I come to the realization

that I reflect you,

in your moments,

of grief and isolation.

Friendship Never Lasts

I don't think it's fair
to judge me for things I can't control,
but I should've known
that "I love you" isn't real
and friendships never last.

I'm Sorry

There are no reasons left for me to feel
like I cannot breathe
but the tension in my body
is a constant reminder of
things I cannot erase.

I still wake up with fear.
It is so spine-chillingly present, and I am without the
comfort of words to keep me sane
how can I sleep when my dreams
want me to disappear?
There is no greater cruelty
than being left alone with my brain.

Remorse has become a tiring expression in my vocabulary
I know you're as tired as I am, but these cruel statements
have become addicting.
They eat me from the inside out, and I've had enough of
their drowning love
I just need a little time a little time, to hold myself down, so
I can be worthy of the words that make me golden

until then, please bear with me, my promise may seem
empty,
but just know, I am sorry.

Martyr

You are the martyr,
stuck inside this treasure bearing my feelings of rancor and
enmity
if it's meant to be, it will be.

For now, I lay still
and amass that which makes me powerful
so, I no longer need my martyr, so I no longer need you.

Walk-In Closet

I want you to feel how I felt
stumbling, wordless
unable to grieve
the life I lost, when you came at night.

The Right Thing

I must be dreaming again because,
this world feels a little different
I wish I knew what I am waiting for
Then, I would know if I was doing
the right thing.

November

These hands that hold me up
mean nothing if I can't speak up.

I am yanked down
by words engraved in my mind
reminding me I am not enough.

I can feel the distance, I yearn for it
it's something illogical, but it's all I can feel.

If you're reading this, will you hold me back when I need
you to?

L.

I want to be dead
today, I took my first breathe
glad, you didn't die.

Nothing

In the late hours of the night
I should have known not to trust it
maybe my mistake was that I gave myself too fast
to a force that could not pull me out
as fast as I would for them.
It feels like a race and the only one loosing is me
bury me here, where my heart can be left to burn
I promise I have nothing left to say.

Are You Listening?

This is the land of the free,
the land of the free…
what freedom is there?
Where is this freedom
when our people are held in shackles
not just our bodies, but our spirits and minds too
what freedom is there,
when our nights are filled with wails of mothers
whose children were unjustifiably murdered,
in the name, of justice,
tell me, where can I find this freedom?
How do we liberate our bodies?
These same bodies, you reject for being too dark or not light
enough
for being too E X O T I C for your taste
tell me, where do I find this freedom?

Rough, Rough, Rough...

As I watch from below,
gently decomposed
in a silver-white gown,
like the mothers before.
Lacking flesh,
with a low hum
thumping through my chambers.
The sound filling the night.

Above me, the sky unfolds
an eternity of dark
time is unyielding
unraveled, yet intertwined
all I get to see
is what lies beneath my feet.

I wait, I wait
for my mind and soul
to be whole.

Octubre

Como quisiera estar en mi lindo hogar
me saboreo el dulce sabor de pan dulce
y el café de olla de mi abuela,
aunque estaba muy pequeña para tomar café.

Extraño el olor del mar acapulceño
el frio del agua que persigue mis pies
en un juego de amor.

Extraño los días largos caminando en la plaza con mis
abuelos y el aroma tan sabroso de los platillos que salen
del tianguis que nunca podía comprar.

Extraño la tierra que me cubre de pies a cabeza
y el camino largo a la casa de luz.
Donde me esperaba una cama compartida y un plato de
frijoles con tortillas hecho a mano.

Extraño la casa gris, aunque siempre estaba
basia y fría.
Extraño a Poppis, mi mejor amigo, que se murió
dormido a mis pies.
Extraño el árbol en donde lo deje descansar.

Extraño mis abuelos y el olor de seguridad.
Extraño el abrazo de mis ancestros, cuando se despidieron
de mí.
Extraño ese último octubre de mi niñez.

Our Bodies

Your reflection remains askew, yet you pay no heed
bones, pale skin
coarse hair.
Are you happy?
Day after day
they shove fabricated perfection in your face
the frenzy intensifies as you impersonate the dolls,
their shells creamy and shiny.
Smooth skin, retouched to conceal the cracks and crevices
bodies pulled left and right, stretched and shrunken.
Elfin-like faces molded by fake gods
this is not a virtual reality.
Your meals are left forgotten on the table
but your skeletal form isn't enough,
your assimilation is futile, and your efforts are wasted.
Hips too wide
nose too large
breasts too small
waist too thick
you search longingly in the mirror,
but only find them.
You've surrendered to the man with the knife

will you sign your name on empty sheets?
And when your dreams are fulfilled, will you wear a mask?
Will you hide your fear and imperfections?

Postcards

Don't you get tired of this
running back and forth?
Looking for a place where growth is allowed, and you're
not stuck all by yourself?

Now, you're in the middle of the room
left thinking about all that you gave
to a man who never bothered to come home.

You're left with nothing to hold but the memories of him
and a stack of old postcards.

Current Exchange

I'm sad, there I said it.
I am so sad, I ran out of ways to say it.
That's it, that's the poem.

June

There's a pain in my chest,
my stomach sinks
I feel sick, my forehead slick with sweat
the door frame is filled with
a faint illusion…

Escaping

Breathe in deeply, now,
pick yourself up.
No one else will help you,
so, you need to save yourself, rely on yourself,
because this world
is a hungry man
and it won't stop until
you've been devoured.

Bad Friend

I can tell by the way you pushed me out
your silence,
like shards of broken glass
into my worn-out heart.
Who am I to decide how you feel?
Who are you to decide who I am?

Love, Child

I promise to keep you safe
I promise to hold you when you cry
I promise to be there when you open your eyes
I promise you, you're brave
I promise I will eat with you,
big stacks of pancakes, just the way you like them.

I haven't seen you in a while, but I know you.
I know who you will be.
I know that I love you unconditionally
I know that I forgive you,
for what I don't know, but I know that I do.
I know you're my favorite part of the day.
I know that you're enough,
you're more than enough.

But I know that you're hurting
and I know that you don't believe me.
I know you've been let down.
I know you've been disappointed
and I know you feel fear.

I know you didn't have a childhood,
I'm sorry you didn't have a childhood.
You are safe now, you are safe,
and I *love you*, child.

Leaving

A slither of light mirrored against the wall
of our somber living room.
You asked me to stay,
did you lose your way again?
The hallway remains empty,
it was too late.

The Way You Hurt

It's an itch, an infection spread all over my body.
The sunlight beams through the same spot
as it does every morning,
illuminating
one miserable corner of my college apartment.
It's itchy, everything is so god damn itchy.
My coffee tastes bland, the seven eleven brands, and the
painting won't stop laughing at me.
It just won't shut up; it won't shut up.
Back and forth
back and forth
I'm pacing the floor, back and forth
scratching, scratching, scratching
itch, itch, itch
I tug up my hair, tug it back down
and everything is still so itchy
the painting laughs harder
now the walls are laughing.
Now the walls are moving

they're moving in! they're moving!
and I can't—
I can't—
I…

they're moving in! they're moving!
and I can't—
I can't—
I…

Sunrise

Smile at yourself
you are worthy of the world
the clouds will go away
you will see the sky one day
one day you will reach a place
made just for you
and you will embrace
and celebrate your light.

Letting Go

One day I will let go
I will take a deep breath
and feel the warm, summer air
hope on the horizon, as the veil breaks
skin shedding, a thousand paper flowers
my feet take off,
a comforting heat beneath me
as snakes unwrap themselves
revealing the marks around my throat.
One day I will let go
of the image of your face,
as it looms above, in the cold dark room.